GRAB | GATHER | GROW

Also available from Jim and Jennifer Cowart

Start This, Stop That

Grab, Gather, Grow

Grab, Gather, Grow: DVD

Living the Five: Participant and Leader Book

Living the Five: DVD

Hand Me Downs: Participant and Leader Book

Hand Me Downs: DVD

Praise for *Grab, Gather, Grow*

"*Grab, Gather, Grow* proves that often the best ideas are not all that complicated. Small groups can be organic rather than forced. They can be missional as well as formational, evangelistic as well as educational. But most of all, they can leverage a congregation's most underutilized asset: its preexisting relationships with people outside the church."

—Magrey R. deVega, Senior Pastor, Hyde Park UMC, Tampa, FL; author, *Awaiting the Already, One Faithful Promise;* leadership editor of Covenant Bible Study

"Jim and Jen Cowart continue to provide resources that can assist local congregations in their discipleship ministries. The Cowarts are among the best spiritual leaders in the church, and their approaches to ministry have come to be very fruitful. The G3 system will help you foster group growth and assimilate new members into the community of faith."

—Lindsey Davis, Bishop, Louisville Episcopal Area, UMC

"Jim and Jennifer have challenged me again to rethink my leadership in *Grab, Gather, Grow*. Innovation combined with a strategic focus on mission is what launches the local church to be a movement that really is helpful, connects people, and facilitates transformation. Thanks for reminding us that change is our friend and God's tool for making disciples of Jesus!"

—Steve Wood, Lead Pastor, Mount Pisgah UMC, Johns Creek, GA

"The G3 concept outlined in this book is not a theory of small groups—it is a proven strategy that's helping churches of all sizes grow their impact and see more lives changed. Church leaders will find it both inspiring and highly actionable."

—Tony Morgan, Founder and Chief Strategic Officer, The Unstuck Group

"Harvest Church is one of the most exciting stories in contemporary United Methodism. No small part of that is the leadership of Jim and Jen Cowart. This book witnesses to that. What they model here is creative, practical, and replicable. I heartily commend it."

—Maxie Dunnam, Director, Christ Church Global; Senior Emeritus, Christ UMC, Memphis, TN

"The Grab, Gather, Grow method is more than just a 'program.' It's a way of structuring your small groups so your church grows healthy. I love what Jim and Jennifer are doing. Churches need to read this book!"

—Steve Gladen, Pastor of Small Groups, Saddleback Church; author, *Small Groups with Purpose*

"In our highly independent culture, living in rich, robust community sounds radical. Yet the Bible and church history sees community as normal for every follower of Jesus. Jim and Jennifer give the church a practical and doable gift in G3 that helps everyone in your church connect to a community group. It can change your life, church, and community."

—Jorge Acevedo, Lead Pastor, Grace Church, a multisite UMC congregation

"The profound simplicity of the G3 strategy is surpassed only by its effectiveness in reaching and connecting people. Jim and Jennifer are masters at making complex matters accessible so that we can all be more effective at grabbing, gathering, and growing people for Christ's kingdom. I highly recommend reading and implementing G3!"

—Bryan D. Collier, Founding and Lead Pastor, The Orchard, Tupelo, MS

GRAB | GATHER | GROW

Multiply Community Groups in Your Church

JIM AND JENNIFER COWART

Abingdon Press™

Nashville

GRAB, GATHER, GROW:
MULTIPLY COMMUNITY GROUPS IN YOUR CHURCH

Copyright © 2016 by Jim and Jennifer Cowart

This book is printed on acid-free paper.

Library of Congress Cataloging-in-Publication Data

Names: Cowart, Jim, author.
Title: Grab, gather, grow : multiply community groups in your church / Jim and Jennifer Cowart.
Description: First [edition]. | Nashville, Tennessee : Abingdon Press, 2016. | Includes bibliographical references.
Identifiers: LCCN 2016019605| ISBN 9781501825057 (pbk.) | ISBN 9781501825064 (epub)
Subjects: LCSH: Church growth. | Communities—Religious aspects—Christianity.
Classification: LCC BV652.25 .C69 2016 | DDC 253/.7—dc23 LC record available at https://lccn.loc.gov/2016019605

ISBN: 978-1-5018-2505-7
DVD ISBN: 978-1-5018-2508-8
Streaming Video ISBN: 978-1-5018-2507-1

16 17 18 19 20 21 22 23 24 25—10 9 8 7 6 5 4 3 2 1
MANUFACTURED IN THE UNITED STATES OF AMERICA

Contents

Acknowledgments

To our friends who have helped to craft both the G3 process and this book:

Teri Nave, Jessi Marlow, Joseph Myers, Pam Floyd, and Brett Eastman.

Grab, Gather, and Grow

Welcome to G3, which is short for *Grab*, *Gather*, and *Grow*. These three verbs are steps to help mobilize your church for tremendous growth. This system will help you achieve not only healthy numeric growth but also growth in discipleship, growth in ministry and mission activity, as well as growth in spiritual relationships. In this book and the accompanying video, you will discover a proven leadership strategy to maximize your results in connecting people in your congregation, community, and beyond through small groups.

For years we have heard prominent Christian leaders say that it is possible to see more people involved in group life during the week than in attendance in worship on the weekend. In fact, they would even go so far as to say that 100 percent participation in groups is not the goal. Instead, the goal is to see upwards of 110 percent of the weekend attendance actively involved in group life. What? Are you kidding? It preaches well at a training event, but is it really possible? Could it just be *seminar rhetoric*? You know what *seminar rhetoric* is, right? It is the things presenters tell you are possible during a training seminar, but the idea of it happening in your local setting seems unattainable. Well, if you've ever experienced *seminar rhetoric,* then you can understand our surprise when we realized that, after adopting a new strategy for group life, we did indeed have more people involved in groups some weeks than we had in worship on the weekend. (And we had good crowds on the weekend!)

Many churches are stuck in patterns that are not yielding the best results. We realized this was true in our setting several years ago, so we hired a coach, Brett Eastman from Life Together ministries, to help us move forward in the area of small group involvement. Through that consultation, we began developing a strategy that has led to tremendous growth spiritually and relationally. This is the strategy we want to share with you through this book. It's called Grab, Gather, and Grow. Feel free to tweak this process, and make it work in your situation! As Christian leaders, our responsibility is not only to feed our sheep but also to equip them and create systems of health and growth so that they, too, can feed sheep. Ideally, these systems need little maintenance once established and can allow for years of growth in many areas. In the early church, we read in Acts:

> A sense of awe came over everyone. God performed many wonders and signs through the apostles. All the believers were united and shared everything. They would sell pieces of property and possessions and distribute the proceeds to everyone who needed them. Every day, they met together in the temple and ate in their homes. They shared food with gladness and simplicity. They praised God and demonstrated God's goodness to everyone. The Lord added daily to the community those who were being saved. (Acts 2:43-47 CEB)

The early church had a system! There was a system for corporate worship in the temple and a system for ministry, fellowship, study, and mission in homes. G3 is a similar system.

This is a how-to book. You already know the theology motivating it from scripture:

Go into the whole world and make disciples . . . (Mark 16:15, paraphrased)

Love each other . . . (John 13:34 CEB)

Carry each other's burdens . . . (Gal 6:2 CEB)

A three-ply cord doesn't easily snap . . . (Eccl 4:12 CEB)

As *iron sharpens iron, so friends sharpen each [other]* . . .
(Prov 27:17 CEB)

Don't stop meeting together with other believers . . . (Heb
10:25 CEB)

Love your neighbor as yourself . . . (Mark 12:31 CEB)

These scriptures, and so many more, point to the need for
us to be in community with each other. They stress the strength
that comes from doing life together with a shared purpose. But
our world, our churches, and our people are already so very
busy. Within the church, we usually attend too many meetings,
accomplish too little ministry, and often feel too much stress.
In fact, in the bustle of life, many of the people in our churches
and community find themselves desperately lonely. So what do
we do? We build a system to help people connect to each other,
to Christ, and into meaningful ministry. Grab, Gather, and Grow
can help you do this!

In our situation, two weeks after beginning G3, we were able
to assimilate more people into groups meeting in homes, busi-
nesses, and restaurants than we had in weekend worship. Even
more surprising and exciting is these small groups are bearing
fruit. Over the past year we have seen a 350 percent increase
in the number of groups offered in our church family. This rep-
resents more than a thousand additional people now engaged
with each other on a weekly basis to study God's word, invite the
lost, engage in missions, take care of each other, and worship
together.

How? This result is accomplished by giving our people an
easy-to-use, video-driven resource provided through our church,
encouraging them to gather a few friends from the community,
and having them commit to growing together in a small group

setting. The video teaching on the DVD is done by a skilled communicator, which allows people who may have been previously intimidated by "teaching" to step into leadership. The gathering is done by the one who grabs the resource, and the growth occurs through the sweet process of inviting God into our lives within these group settings.

In some ways, by allowing all church members to grab a resource, the qualification bar for leadership is lowered. The average church attendee is able to step into a leadership role and reach out to his or her circle of friends and family outside the church family. This is a part of the secret sauce for G3. By equipping the people of God with high-quality materials and then encouraging them to reach out to those they know outside the church walls, we have been able to reach many more people with the love and message of Christ.

Many of our peers, with varying demographics—geography, style of worship, and size—experience similar results. For example, our friend Jeff, a pastor in Ohio, implemented a version of the G3 process with great results. Five months after introducing this strategy, his congregation moved from 180 people involved in eighteen groups to more than 500 people involved in forty-seven groups, and they are still growing.

After just two series, David, a pastor in Texas, experienced a similar outcome. His church added fifty groups. These are both relatively large churches. However, the system works in all locations and is effective with varying demographics. A smaller church trying this approach added seven groups. It sounds small in comparison until you realize this doubled their attendance. Don't be overwhelmed by the numbers. Scale the process to your situation.

But think exponentially and not incrementally!

We are excited to share this process with you because we believe that it will work for you no matter the size or location of

your congregation. And as it works, you will ultimately be able to reach more people with the love and message of Christ. In fact, as you unleash the power of encouraging everyone to reach out to those in their spheres of influence, the stories that emerge will amaze you.

With more than three hundred groups now meeting in and beyond our church community, we hear stories almost daily about what God is doing among our people. Many of these stories are about people who never attended a Bible study before. But by grabbing a resource and gathering their friends, they are now growing together in Christ.

In another example, we received a note from a participant, Tamera, who shared with us that simply by grabbing a resource and using it with friends from her work setting, she made an impact on a very unique population. Tamera works with adults who have special needs, including several who are nonverbal. After viewing a resource on love, she invited small groups of her clients into her home and did the study with them.

This group, like so many others, is one we would never have envisioned. But by loosening the constraints of who is qualified to lead and by empowering our attendees to invite, we are seeing tremendous growth both within the community and in who is being reached.

As we dig into the strategy of G3, we pray that the Holy Spirit will begin to open your eyes, as the Spirit opened our eyes and Tamera's eyes, to all the possibilities in front of you!

CHAPTER 1
The Role of Leadership

Now, the fact that you have this material and are reading it tells us something very important about you. You are a leader. You have the opportunity to make an impact on the lives of others. And it's our guess that you want to be as faithful as you can be with that privilege and responsibility. We believe the G3 strategy of assimilation and study will help you to do that.

Effective leaders are constantly innovating. They are always looking for the most effective ways to accomplish their goals.

The Uber Analogy by Carey Niewhouf

For instance, let's take a look at the amazing rise of Uber, a ride-hail company similar to a taxi service but that works off an app. This company, originating out of San Francisco, took over a major portion of the market share of cab revenue before most of the population even knew what it was about. Uber has disrupted—with a good bit of controversy—the taxi industry, which has operated basically in the same fashion for almost one hundred years. How does that happen, and what can the church learn from it?

Carey Niewhouf cites seven key learnings for the church from the lesson of Uber.[1]

---

1. Carey Nieuwhof, "What the Church Can Learn from the Astounding Rise of Uber," *Carey Nieuwhof* (blog), February 4, 2016, http://careynieuwhof.com/2016/02/what-the-church-can-learn-from-the-rise-of-uber/.

1. OWNING A GREAT TAXI CAB IS NO LONGER ENOUGH.

In an age where everyone used taxis, having a clean cab, or a slightly less expensive cab, or a larger fleet of cabs that provided quick service was a competitive advantage. Not so when an industry gets disrupted. Uber uses ordinary people's cars and allows users to rate drivers for their friendliness and cooperation. And they offer [a] price that's meaningfully below a typical cab ride. In the age of Uber, you can have the best taxi cab in town and still be out of business.

What can church leaders learn from this? Polishing a current model of ministry to make it better often comes at the expense of true innovation.

2. INNOVATION DOESN'T ASK FOR APPROVAL.

Uber innovated in three primary areas that the taxi industry never did: they lowered the price, enlisted anyone who wanted to drive as a driver and gave consumers the ability to instantly call a car via their phones.

Are there problems with Uber? Sure . . . many think Uber needs some regulation. But that's not the point. The point is they already won real market share before most people even knew what was happening. Uber is a great example of how innovation changes things rapidly. Cities and the taxi industry are catching up with Uber long after the love affair between many consumers and Uber began. This is a note to denominations and even churches with large bureaucracies.

Innovation doesn't ask for approval. It just happens— much to the annoyance of existing power structures, which tend to be about preserving what has been.

3. FIGHTING CHANGE DOESN'T STOP CHANGE.

It's rather surprising to see how angry and opposed taxi cab owners have become in their opposition to Uber.

Their opposition has even spilled to violence on the streets. This is nothing new. The Luddites famously fought the invention of motorized textile looms, smashing and burning the new technology. They lost.

Fighting change doesn't stop change. The best leaders see change and adapt to it, never compromising the mission but reinventing the methods (which is exactly what Uber is doing). Complaining about change doesn't change anything either.

4. WHEN YOU CONFUSE METHOD WITH MISSION, YOU LOSE.

Taxi cabs have been a *method* of temporary transportation for a century. But the mission behind the taxi industry is *transportation*. Uber never mistook the method for the mission. It appears that the taxi industry has done just that. We *all* get wedded to our methods . . . The church is seriously in danger of confusing method with mission.

The cab industry could have become innovative and pioneered Uber-like service and innovation. But it didn't. When someone came along with a more popular method, they grew defensive. Now it looks like the cab industry is far more wedded to their method than they are to their mission.

Know any churches like that?

5. YOUR PAST SUCCESS IS NO GUARANTEE OF YOUR FUTURE SUCCESS.

Having the best cab fleet of the 21st century may not matter as much as it did 5 years ago. Your past success is no guarantee of your future success. Not in the face of innovation and disruption. The best way to ensure future success is to keep experimenting and keep innovating.

When was the last time your church innovated?

6. INNOVATION SPAWNS MORE INNOVATION, WHILE DEFENSIVENESS SPAWNS DEATH.

Very little has changed in the cab industry in the last few decades. Sure, payments have become mobile and now there are TVs in some cabs (but again, TV is hardly a new invention). Uber was only an *idea* as recently as 2009. It launched its first service in 2010. But as young as Uber is, it has introduced black car services, car-pooling, transit and is experimenting with fresh food delivery, package delivery and so much more.

That's because an innovative culture spawns more innovation.

Meanwhile, as outlined above, the taxi industry's main response is not innovation, but a demand that Uber go away. Uber isn't going away any time soon. And even if Uber disappears, innovation won't.

Church leaders, take note. Innovation spawns more innovation. Defensiveness spawns death. So start innovating.

7. SELF-INTEREST WILL INEVITABLY LOSE TO PUBLIC INTEREST.

The church should be the least self-interested organization in the world. When we behave this way, the mission will grow.

If you watch the taxi industry's response to Uber, you can't help but conclude that the stance they've taken seems self-interested. I realize these are people who need jobs and money to feed their families, but their arguments come across as self-motivated.

Ever notice that selfishness and defensiveness are only attractive to the person being selfish and defensive?

Through lower prices, friendly service and convenience, Uber's winning the PR war because it *feels* like it's on the consumer's side.

Uber has problems for sure (its drivers have already gone on strike), but the difference between the vibe Uber emits and the vibe the cab industry emits is significant.

Self-interest will always lose to the public interest.

Let's bring this analogy to the G3 system. This is a new strategy. It requires innovation. The mission is timeless, but the methods are new. So as we go through this material and you come to a moment during which you think, *This just won't work in our setting* or *We won't be able to get people to buy into this*, remember the lesson from Uber. Don't be the angry taxicab driver!

In the church, we need great, innovative leaders. We yearn for leaders who not only have vision but also can share that vision in a clear and compelling way that motivates people to action. The people of God are hungry for leaders who will stand up boldly and lead them. They need pastors and leaders who will equip them so they can take on their roles in effective and fulfilling ways.

In a letter circulated to the early churches, Jesus becomes the source who authorizes the primary responsibility of those in leadership, "He gave some apostles, some prophets, some evangelists, and some pastors and teachers. His purpose was to equip God's people for the work of serving and building up the body of Christ" (Eph 4:11-12 CEB).

The primary responsibility of the pastor is to lead! However, all too often pastors spend the majority of their time doing the hired-holy-stuff, such as visiting the sick, counseling the troubled, and attending lots of meetings. These are important tasks, but they are tasks that laity could do effectively. If the pastor and staff are consumed with these tasks, it leaves very little energy for leadership.

The biblical model looks like this: Pastors cast vision and then train and equip believers. In other words, the pastor and staff are administrators and leaders. The laity *do* the ministry. G3 helps facilitate this process.

However, even strong leaders find that as they try to innovate, they encounter challenges. We understand because we too have experienced many obstacles, including opposition, minimal funding, and a lack of leadership.

No matter the size of your church, your location, or your demographics, this G3 process can work for you. Yet there may be obstacles to overcome. We have experienced them also. Will you be a leader who overcomes challenges?

Are you a "so" person or a "but" person? All leaders come against obstacles. Here are just a few:

We'd like to grow, **but** . . .

I'd be glad to serve, **but** . . .

That may work there, **but** . . .

We could try it, **but** . . .

Every church is full of big buts (pun intended). As a leader, you should guide the conversation from "but" to "so":

We'd like to grow, **so** we have to try some new ways of reaching the community.

I need some people to serve, **so** I'm going to have lunch with a few key leaders.

Leaders move past the big buts in their congregations to solve things through the power of "so."

Whatever your confronting issues, take a breath and think about how you will engineer the desirable changes. We have a phrase we often use with our church staff and our children: "engineer your win." In other words, figure it out. Have the meeting before the meeting. Troubleshoot in advance in order to reach the goals of ministry. Pray. Fast. Seek guidance. Hire a coach. Do the hard work to gather all your information. Be positive. Take the steps necessary to make it happen. This is what it means to "engineer your win."

One of the obstacles we faced early in ministry was how to start a church. We had a big dream of reaching people far from God in a new community, **but** we had no people, no land, no leadership team, and little money. **So**, in order to "engineer the win," we invited friends from an hour away to attend our first services. We knew that they would not be able to worship with us on a weekly basis long term, but as we launched into a new community, we needed friendly people who were willing to serve as greeters, musicians, child care and cleanup workers, and so on. At our first service we were thrilled to have 150 people in attendance. However, more than seventy-five of them were friends from other communities who had come in to help us get started. Their attendance in those early services gave us tremendous manpower and enthusiasm to start strong.

We also struggled with obstacles in trying to grow our small-group ministry. Even with a full-time staff, we had not been able to get beyond seventy-five groups. Most churches find barriers in growth that are difficult to break through. In our group system, seventy-five was that barrier. And most likely, whether your current system is Sunday school, a midweek ministry, or small groups throughout the week, you have probably faced some obstacles and growth barriers.

As we were looking to make a staff change in our small-group ministry, we talked with a friend who said, "You're asking the wrong question. Instead of asking *Who?* ask *What?* Change the strategy and see what happens." This is where Grab, Gather, and Grow came into play. Instead of looking for a new staff person to implement the same old structure, we needed new structure. Then we could consider what type of staffing needed to be in place to implement the new system. But first, we needed a new system.

It's important to note the word *system* here. The G3 process is not a program or a study. It's a discipleship process and a growth system. There's a big difference between church programs and church pro-

ALERT

IF YOU TREAT THE G3 PROCESS AS A PROGRAM, YOU WILL EXPERIENCE TEMPORARY RESULTS. INSTEAD, TREAT IT AS A FUNDAMENTAL SHIFT IN HOW SMALL GROUPS ARE DONE IN YOUR SETTING. IT IS A SYSTEM FOR CONTINUALLY ENGAGING ALL PARTICIPANTS IN GROUP LIFE THROUGHOUT THE YEAR, WHATEVER THE SERMON TOPIC OR WORSHIP SEASON.

cesses. On the one hand, with a program or study, you do it once and you're done. A system, on the other hand, sets up a structure for continual growth. G3 is a process to help you build a disciple-making system that becomes part of the DNA of your congregation. It becomes part of how ministry is done in your setting.

The system of developing smaller groups within and beyond the church stems from the model we see in Acts 2. The early church met together in the temple courts. But it also met in smaller gatherings from house to house. Throughout scripture, we read about how important it is to do life together. We read about praying for one another, loving one another, and encouraging one another, just to name a few. The best place to live life with each other is in a smaller setting, where we can really do life together.

The G3 system is not a process to delegate. It is led from the pulpit by the lead pastor. Often in ministry, we are taught or advised to delegate responsibilities. It is a helpful way to multiply ministries in a congregation. But when you want to share new ideas and get the entire congregation involved, it is always the responsibility of the lead pastor to cast the vision.

If your church has someone, whether on staff or a layperson, who is responsible for the group system, he or she will need to be involved in an integral way. But the role of vision casting is best done from the pulpit. The primary tasks of the staff and lay volunteer is to develop a system for deploying materials, following up with facilitators, troubleshooting issues within the group, and helping groups find mission projects. But it is not their job to cast the vision or get people into groups.

When the lead pastor gets behind the Grab, Gather, and Grow process and weaves it into the DNA of how the church operates, including making it part of the weekend messages, it legitimizes the system. Everyone knows this is who we are and this is where we are going.

One of the questions that must be settled as you move into the G3 process is well-known in the world of groups: "Are we a church *with* groups or *of* groups?" There is a vast difference between the two. The church *with* groups has value in making Bible study part of the menu of program offerings within the church body. The church *of* groups makes it clear that all attendees need to be part of a group in order to live out the Great Commandment and Great Commission in community. When the lead pastor repeatedly casts the vision of being a church of groups, it sets a clear expectation and empowers the process.

As you cast this vision of having 100 percent and more of your attendees engaged in groups, do it with confidence and enthusiasm. It really is happening at churches all around the country, and yours could be next!

CHAPTER 2

Defining the Three G's

In chapter 4 we will take you step-by-step through the process of implementing the G3 process. But first, let's break down the process into three simple steps. The simplicity of the process is actually a key to the success of the whole strategy!

As you communicate to the general congregation, here are the three essentials you want them to know and do:

(1) Grab a resource.

(2) Gather a few friends.

(3) Grow together through the upcoming series.

Keep it that simple. People are more likely to buy into new ways of doing things when the process is understandable and clear.

Grab – Invite your attendees to grab a free DVD and printed resource to guide a small group. This process typically begins two weeks before the launch of a new message series and continues through the first week or two of that message series. The lead pastor invites everyone in the congregation to take the resource, *as a gift*, in exchange for being willing to gather a few friends and grow through this series. The materials work best when designed as a supplement to the weekend message.

By having materials readily available after a worship service (or other gathering), you lower the bar for leadership, allowing everyone to participate as a host. This will exponentially expand the pool of people you may be able to reach during the gather-and-grow stage.

In larger congregations with media staff, if time and resources allow, you may want to create these video-based teaching materials in-house. However, this step is not necessary. For example, as a smaller congregation, when preparing to purchase land, we used John Ortberg's study *If You Want to Walk on Water* as our small-group resource. We coupled it with weekend messages about faith and generosity. It worked really well because it fit the challenging context in the life of our faith community.

It is possible to adapt various short-term video-based studies to fit the G3 process. Other video studies we have used in a church-wide series include *The Dream Giver* by Bruce Wilkerson; *The Purpose Driven Life* by Rick Warren; and *Life's Healing Choices* by John Baker.

Materials are now being developed, at a much-reduced cost to the participating congregation, so that it is affordable for churches of all sizes to purchase community group studies in bulk quantities. To implement the G3 process, the resources should be provided so that community groups can multiply at an exponential rate. For example, Abingdon Press (our publisher) is aiming to distribute video-based studies at a discounted cost under five dollars for each video disk (and under ten dollars for each discounted participant/leader guide), which is supplied by the church to each community group during the "grab the resource" step. By planning ahead and coupling the weekend message, the G3 process will work with most biblical video-based curriculum or small-group studies.

Gather – Immediately after grabbing a resource, hosts are encouraged to reach out and invite churched and especially non-churched friends, neighbors, and coworkers to join them for the study. Encourage hosts to meet in homes, offices, and even restaurants and parks. The intent is to move the setting outside of the church walls and into neutral settings. A familiar setting may help those far from God to be more comfortable. During this time, those who have grabbed a resource need to be encouraged to reach out to as many people as they comfortably can, so they are able to fill their groups and experience a positive group launch.

Grow – This begins as soon as the group assembles. In the G3 system, the traditional small-group emphasis of fellowship and discipleship is expanded to include evangelism, ministry, and worship. By intentionally having groups develop balance as they live into the Great Commission and Great Commandment, the result will be healthier groups. And healthy things grow.

CHAPTER 3

Key Components to Success

The Importance of Balance

Most small groups do at least two things well—fellowship and Bible study. However, at their best, they can be so much more!

Group life is a great way to live out the Great Commandment and Great Commission in community. As Rick Warren points out in the Purpose Driven Church Strategy, the five purposes for Christian life together are worship, evangelism, discipleship, fellowship, and ministry. A key component to the overall health and success of G3 is balancing these five areas. This is so important to the church family that we have implemented community groups through a launch resource, with the phrase *Living the Five*, which means living intentionally into each of these purposes.

All groups are encouraged in every gathering to incorporate these five habits:

- **Evangelism**—inviting new people to join the group

- **Fellowship**—caring for one another emotionally, spiritually, and physically

- **Ministry**—taking on a mission project either in the church or in the community

- **Worship**—praying and possibly even singing together

- **Discipleship**—studying God's word and applying it to life together

The benefits to this balance are numerous. For instance, our need for membership care from staff and pastors has diminished greatly because the people are caring for each other. This frees the staff to spend more time equipping laypeople for ministry and preparing for the weekend services. By having more than three hundred groups actively seeking ways to engage in ministry opportunities in our church and community during each study, we are able, as the body of Christ, to do so much more than we could through a single church-wide emphasis.

One of our community groups—a small group of women—meets weekly to prepare backpacks for children who do not have enough food each weekend. As part of their weekly gathering, they stuff seventy-two packs for at-risk children in our area. Another community group prepares and distributes hygiene kits for the homeless. These projects are completely autonomous. The groups handle everything themselves, including coordination and funding. At Christmas, for the past few years, we have gathered together with our community group hosts to hear their outreach stories. It is overwhelming to hear of projects, which range from malaria vaccines to tutoring, being planned and done by these community groups!

The emphasis on inviting those far from God to join the groups also helps the church reach out with the good news. Through the G3 process, community groups attract many people who have not yet come to corporate worship. In other words, they have not attended church yet, but they are meeting weekly in homes with their friends to learn more. This is great! And it helps our people live out the Great Commission.

The Approach to Community

As you approach the G3 system, consider expanding your thinking about what group life can look like. Instead of thinking about Bible study, cell group, or small group, we encourage you to use the label *community group*. The word *community* implies that the group is open to everyone in your area, the entire community. In our culture the church may not always seem open to everyone even though we may mean for it to be open. For people who don't attend your church, they may not know if they are really welcome to come in your doors or participate in your groups.

The use of the word *community* has been so beneficial to changing our church culture, in fact, that we now use it in most of our church advertising. For example, invitational cards and billboards may read: "You're invited to a Community Christmas Celebration." For people far from God, it gives them permission to belong.

The term *community* also opens up our groups to a wider audience. Recently, during our membership class, we met a woman who had never been to church before. Yet, there she was, in a two-hour course about what it means to be a member of the family of God and part of a congregation. Curious, right? She explained that she had been attending a community group at a neighbor's home and found it to be life changing. When she was told about the membership class, she wanted to hear more about the church. After meeting us, she said, "Who knows? Maybe next week I'll even come to hear you preach."

Some people aren't ready to come through the doors for worship. But they may be open to going over to their neighbor's home one night a week for snacks and a video-based lesson. And if that is a positive experience, it might be their first step toward a relationship with Christ.

While Jen was shopping recently, she met a delightful woman who stopped and said, "Hey, you're the woman that leads my community group."

So she replied, "Oh, do you come to Harvest?" The woman replied, "Oh no. I don't go to church, but I do go to my neighbor's house for Bible study. You're that woman on the screen, right?" Jen introduced herself, listened to a little of her story, and then told her that when and if she got ready to try out a service, Jen would be one of the people ready to greet her.

By simply adding the word *community*, a great deal is communicated. The outside-in point of view lets those who have doubts and questions know that "yes, you are invited."

The Release of Control

It's a difficult lesson to learn, but great leaders know that *you can structure for control or growth, but you simply cannot have both.* This has been one of the harder but more meaningful lessons for us to learn over the years. As you will see, as we get into the process of G3, anyone (really, anyone) is allowed to grab a resource and gather friends for the community groups.

Because the biblical teaching is delivered by a skilled biblical communicator through a DVD resource, you don't have to worry about the quality of the teaching. The people who take the materials from the table are not teachers.

This is crucial to the G3 system!

The hosts don't lead the actual study; the DVD video leads the study. The hosts are friends and neighbors who get together with people they know to do life together and explore God's word. By lowering the bar in terms of their preparation and expertise, more people are able to engage.

This may be a struggle for you because as a leader, if you are like us, you may have gotten stuck on quality control. Many churches require a great deal of training before activating people into the role of a host. This seems like the right thing to do, unless it is limiting your effectiveness in advancing the purposes of God's kingdom. If we aren't careful we can develop a culture in which only a few people are "qualified" to do ministry. Has that happened in your church? Do only a few people lead Sunday school or ministry teams? In our day and time, with access to so much technology, we can harness mature teaching and put it into the hands of new seekers and less-mature believers.

Remember who followed Jesus? Primarily, it was ordinary people. Jesus *trusted them* with the message of the gospel. The G3 system follows that example and allows you to put good materials into the hands of your people, some of whom may even be far from God.

But, to be honest, when we first started the G3 system, we were nervous about loosening control. You see, we know some of our folk. We love them! But some of them are sketchy. Do you know the term *sketchy*? It means questionable. Our anxiety centered on what would happen if we put materials into Mr. Sketchy's hands. Well, let us tell you what happened. Mr. Sketchy invited his sketchy buddies, and they got together and *studied the Bible*! In some cases, for the very first time. That's a good thing, friends.

We can structure our churches and ministries for control or growth, but you simply cannot have both.

In our situation, we were stuck at 72 adult groups. But by trying the G3 system, in one week we went from 72 to 226 groups active in our community. We immediately found that people were willing to be in a group. They were interested. They weren't too busy. They just needed a system that worked for them where they were.

Remember: don't say *but;* keep thinking *so*. Consider the possibilities before you get stuck on your obstacles. By controlling the quality of the prepared material, we opened up the potential of who could be hosts in our area. We don't call these people teachers; they are simply hosts. They are inviters, and their network of invitation is far greater than ours is without them.

One young adult who grabbed materials came up to us and said, "You know I'm an unwed mom, and I've always been too shy to show up at a group. I didn't know what people would say about me and the mistakes I've made. Would it be okay if I grabbed one of the resources and got together with some friends, and we did this together?" Yes, absolutely. So now there are eight young women meeting regularly to seek God and study his word, aiming to live life in a new way.

Again, friends, that's a good thing!

When people are given responsibility and begin to build relationships, their pronouns begin to change. They begin to see the ministry of the church as *theirs*, not just *yours*. They begin to think about what *they can do*, instead of what *you need to do*. This is a powerful shift.

By allowing anyone (really, anyone) who is willing to grab a resource and gather a few friends to take the materials, we had to rethink our ideas of how to do ministry and who can be involved. But we've found that by providing solid biblical materials, we are not giving an endorsement to any questionable behaviors people may have. We are simply saying, "Here; try this. We think it will help you and the people you invite."

We also know that by loosening the constraints of who our inviters are, we are more likely to reach people far from God. To use the fisherman metaphor, the net gets cast into much deeper waters than just what the highly qualified church folk may be able to reach on the surface.

You may be like us and need to stop here and reread this section, perhaps several times. Most of us have structured our ministry with high control. This need often comes from a good and well-meaning heart, but it limits our ability to reach people who need God. Again, you can structure for growth or for control, but you cannot have both.

The Power of Synergy

One of the keys to the success of the G3 system is to tie the community group materials to what is taught on the weekend. In other words, the community group materials and the message from the sermon are closely related. By creating additional material and creative questions for dialogue, you get several benefits:

(1) It is easier for people to interact because they have already been introduced to the topic through the weekend sermon. Therefore, they are more likely to contribute to conversation.

(2) It develops synergy within the community by giving your congregation a common theme to talk about. For instance, when they hear that a series is coming up about family, they know that both the weekend and the weekday groups will be on this topic. It sparks conversation in the community.

(3) It becomes easier for your church to advertise what's coming next. The congregation knows that when we have a G3 series, the community group materials and the message will be linked. It becomes easy for them to invite their friends because they can cast vision based on the advertising we put into their hands.

(4) It is much easier to cast vision from the platform or pulpit and communicate the topic to our church and into the community by tying the group materials to the weekend message.

(5) It drives people from community groups to the weekend worship experience. Many times we only think about how we can drive people from the weekend service into groups. However, the G3 system can also drive people *to* the weekend worship experience from their community group. Since they have interest in the study, they are more likely to show up for worship to hear more on the topic.

As we go through the G3 process you will see that selecting sermon topics and group materials that complement each other will help the process run smoothly.

CHAPTER 4

Building the G3 Infrastructure

Step #1: Design Your G3 Strategy

We expect that you are beginning to see the possibilities of this innovative approach to group life. As you begin to dream about your own setting, take the time to develop your church's overall strategy. To assist you in that journey, here are a few questions to consider:

When and how often will we offer the G3 system?

This small-group assimilation strategy is not designed to be used every week of the year. People need a sabbath, even from group life. They also need to have the freedom, on a regular basis, to choose their own curriculum based on the interests and needs within their group.

In general, we recommend doing a church-wide study twice a year, allowing space for rest between the studies. Most church leaders choose two of the following three seasons to introduce campaigns in their church. We suggest choosing two:

· the beginning of the year

· immediately following Easter

· fall, when school starts back

Usually you will spread these semesters out through the year. However, when you first introduce the G3 system it may be helpful to do two campaigns back-to-back to help establish this as a system and not as a onetime program.

What materials will be used?

Spend a little time to do the research about DVD or video-driven studies that are current, affordable, and relevant to your congregation. There are many gifted biblical communicators putting out small-group studies through a video format. Once the topic and resource are selected, the weekend messages and the worship environment can be designed to accompany and lead the series.

To help you get started in a strong way, we encourage you to launch with the community-group resource *Living the Five*. It is a five-week study designed to launch the G3 system, and it is based on the Great Commandment and Great Commission. The five principles highlighted are evangelism, discipleship, ministry, worship, and fellowship. These are also the basics of healthy group life, so this experience helps build healthy DNA into your community groups right from the start. An excerpt from the participant guide is found in the appendix to this book you are reading.

A follow-up resource is *Hand Me Downs*, which is also designed to be used with the G3 system. Both are available through bookstores, including Cokesbury.com. These relatively inexpensive resources will make it easier for the church to absorb the costs of distribution as the strategy is launched.

Who will order materials and in what quantities?

It may be helpful to have one person responsible for material acquisition and distribution and another person responsible for follow-up. Be sure to plan optimistically with your orders. It would be better to have materials left over than not to have enough materials to place in the hands of those willing to step forward.

How, when, and where will materials be distributed?

Two weeks prior to the series launch, have materials available as people exit the worship service. Then continue to make them available until week three of the study. This is the perfect time and place to collect host information also. The host card asks for basic contact information. The easier it is to fill out, the more likely people are to complete it.

GRAB | GATHER | GROW

HOST CONTACT FORM

Name _____

E-mail _____

Phone _____

Returning Host ☐   New Host ☐

Who will follow up with those willing to Grab resources?

It is crucial to have someone, whether a volunteer or staff person, who is responsible for following up in a timely way with those who grab a resource and agree to host. Timely, in our setting, is a goal of contacting each host within forty-eight hours of grabbing the resource. Having someone available to answer questions, offer encouragement, and troubleshoot group issues will boost the confidence of those willing to step out in faith and host.

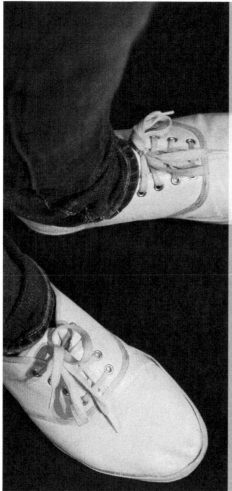

Having someone available to answer questions, offer encouragement, and troubleshoot group issues will boost the confidence of those willing to step out in faith and host.

How will we fund the resources that will be distributed?

We suggest that you give the G3 materials to those willing to host. Your gift of the materials communicates the value you place on recruiting leadership. We strongly encourage you to think of the investment in materials as a church investment in both discipleship and evangelism. It is a gift to those who are willing to host, in return for their offer to gather and grow with others. Ordering and selling extra participant guides for those participating by invitation can help offset the costs associated with the materials for those willing to grab and gather.

Will these groups be hosted on campus or solely in homes and business settings?

Depending on your church tradition, you will need to navigate this question in light of your own culture. If Sunday school, which is discussed in the last section of the book, is a big part of your church structure, then you will need to decide whether those classes continue with their regular studies or whether you choose (perhaps twice a year) to have them do the G3 community group studies.

However, if you yearn to have unchurched people join these community groups, the Sunday school setting does not lend itself to reaching unchurched seekers or de-churched skeptics. The same is true of midweek services. Therefore, you may want to allow the traditional forms of study to continue and introduce the G3 community groups in new environments.

Step #2: Cast the Vision

Pastor, you're up! Take advantage of the pulpit to cast a compelling vision of how this new community-group system will allow your congregation to reach more people for Christ and grow your church. Here's an example of what we might say to our congregation in the weeks leading up to the launch of a new G3 series:

> In two weeks we will begin a new series called *Living the Five*. During these five weeks we're going to dig into the five primary components of Jesus' teaching from the Great Commandment and the Great Commission.
>
> Here's how we want you to get involved. We have tables set up as you exit today with DVDs and participant guides. These are our gift to you if you are willing to **Grab** the materials, **Gather** a few friends, and then **Grow** with us during this new series.
>
> Friends, you can do this. There are people you will meet this week in your neighborhood, at work, in the grocery store, and at school who need to know that Jesus loves them. Invite them to join you. **Grab** a resource set, **Gather** a few friends, and let's **Grow** together.

This is a clear and direct request.

Have you noticed that people usually say no to requests that are not clear? It's usually because they are nervous about over-committing their time.

Generic requests leave too many questions unanswered.

Instead, make the request or the invitation specific. Tell people exactly what you want them to do:

> We want you to **Grab** a free resource as a gift. Then, **Gather** some friends to join you for the next five or six weeks as we **Grow** together. You can gather at your home, business, before school, or wherever you are comfortable. The teaching will be done for you on the DVD, so your responsibility is simply to invite some people, perhaps serve some chips and dip, and guide them through a few questions provided in the participant guide. That's it. You can do this.

In that invitation you've told them:

(1) where to get the materials

(2) what it costs, which is nothing

(3) how long the commitment is, which is just a few weeks

(4) who will be there, which is completely up to whom they invite

We have been shocked at how many people have responded positively to this clear "ask."

If you find that some are having trouble coming up with a list of friends to gather, you can help them start their list. You could suggest something such as: "Think about who you would invite to your Super Bowl party, or to your child's birthday party, or to a book club. Now, write those names down. You've just begun your list. It's that simple."

Make your "ask" simple and clear. Provide a bit of help to start their imaginations, and turn them loose. To ensure that you have a successful start, you can also ask a few people ahead of time to take a copy, review it, and talk it up among their friends. This will help ensure a strong launch. Remember, the key here is to cast a big, clear vision and be positive.

In addition to the lead pastor casting vision, have as many key leaders as possible sharing detailed information about how the system will work. Get people involved. Help them take ownership of the process.

Step #3: Grab the Resource

In your initial planning stages, you will have selected the resource to use that corresponds with the weekend message. If you find a great video-based (DVD) study on the family, then gear the preaching toward Ephesians or Deuteronomy. If the small-group study is on Genesis, then craft messages about fresh starts and new creations. You get the idea. Then make the community-group resources available to anyone willing to Grab a copy, Gather a few friends, and Grow.

We actually place tables in the lobby of our building with stacks of the resources. We give a copy to anyone willing to grab the resource, gather a few friends, and grow during the upcoming series. All we ask from them is to fill out a simple card with their names and contact information. We then are able to encourage them, help them troubleshoot group problems, and keep them engaged when the next study comes around.

Think big as you plan for the Grab stage of the process. It would be tragic to underestimate the demand for materials, which means you have people who are willing to host but not able to participate because of lack of available materials. Remember, the goal is not merely to get 100 percent participation within the church. The G3 goal is to reach outside the church, also building participation over 100 percent!

So let's break that down with simple math. If you have a church of one hundred people in weekend worship, don't order ten sets of the resource, thinking they will have ten participants each. Order twenty-five to thirty-five sets and ask every family to take one and host their own group with their unchurched friends, family, neighbors, and coworkers. This gives the potential for reaching as many as 250–350 in group life.

Surely, at some point the question of how to fund these resources will arise. We really cannot stress strongly enough that for those who host the community-group studies, this G3 strategy works best as a gift. It is an investment in evangelism and discipleship. If people attending, but not hosting, the community groups would like a participant guide, make it easy for them to pay for their materials. By giving the hosts their materials as a gift, you have a certain buy-in that really pays off for your congregation.

The first time we rolled this strategy out to our congregation we used the *Living the Five* resource. Our fifteen-year-old son came to us and said, "There isn't a group meeting for teens that fits in with my football schedule. What do you want me to do?" Now in our home there are a few givens. We are polite, we go to church, we volunteer in a ministry weekly, and we are a part of a community group. So our son, Josh, knew he needed a group. So we suggested that he Grab, Gather, and Grow.

He grabbed the DVD and study guide for *Living the Five*, and he invited the offensive line from his team to our home every Tuesday evening, where he hosted and led them through the discussion. All he wanted from us was pizza for his buddies. Josh's story is a great example of the G3 process because the boys who gathered were not in other Bible studies. One of the guys was not in church at the time, but now he is!

Step #4: Follow Up with Hosts

For many people, stepping out and grabbing a resource may be a huge act of courage. It is important to follow up with them quickly for encouragement and to address any concerns they may have. This is a typical letter that can be sent within forty-eight hours of the church receiving a host card:

Hi friends,

We are so proud of you for stepping out on faith and agreeing to gather with a friend or two to study God's word during our series, _____. You can do this! And we will be here to help if you need us! This particular study may lead you and your group members to questions. Please shoot those queries to us at info@harvestchurch4u .org, and we will address the most common questions in the sermons each week.

The community group process is easy to start with the Grab, Gather, and Grow system. You have already grabbed the free gift of the curriculum. Now continue to invite some people to join you. Healthy, sustainable groups usually have about eight to sixteen regular attenders. So begin inviting and praying for your group!

Here are a few tips to help you have a great experience:

· Review the materials in advance, and select a few questions for discussion.

· Pray for your group time and the members of your group.

· Serve a few refreshments to break the ice and get people socializing.

- Take on a mission project together: locally, nationally, or globally—you choose and implement.

- Take care of each other and have fun!

Remember, we are here to help you! If you have questions, just give the church office a call, or you can reach out to our Community Group staff at info@harvestchurch4u.org.

We love you guys.

Jim and Jen

In addition to this letter, we make phone calls to new hosts and offer occasional socials for everyone to get together. Those hosts who need additional care tend to reach out to us. However, most hosts are content and rarely need much support. The materials are self-explanatory, and unless a personal issue within the group arises, the groups tend to function autonomously.

Providing a simple checklist such as "Ten Tips for the Community Group Host" can also help group hosts get started on the right track.

Ten Tips for the Community Group Host

1. **Relax!** Now, breathe! You can do this, and we're here to help if you get stuck. Remember, God is with you. Pray up, prepare, and be friendly. You can do this! See Hebrews 13:5.

2. **Invite.** Now invite some more people to join you. You are the key to filling your group.

3. **Serve** a few snacks. Food helps break the ice. Keep it simple and then share this responsibility weekly with your group members.

4. **Prepare** for your time together. Preview the DVD, write down your thoughts, and select questions that you feel will work best in your group.

5. **Pray** for your group members. Follow up with them during the week about the concerns in their lives. Make prayer and reaching out to God a regular part of group life.

6. **Maintain** a healthy atmosphere. Don't allow anyone, including you, to dominate discussion or fall into gossip. Redirect gently when conversation deviates.

7. **Share** responsibilities. Asking questions, hosting, bringing snacks, and planning the social and mission project are tasks that can be shared among the group. Don't feel you have to do it all.

8. **Allow silence**. When you ask questions, if there is silence for a moment, don't jump in too quickly to rescue. This may just be a sign that people are thoughtful before responding.

9. Tackle a mission project together! How can you and your group make a difference in the world? Do it!

10. **Have fun**! Plan to do something together outside of the group time just for fun. It helps build friendships and makes the journey more enjoyable!

Step #5: Gather the Crowd

Steps 4 and 5 happen simultaneously. Send the follow-up letter and make phone calls during the same time period that hosts are inviting their friends and neighbors. Some hosts are charismatic and confident and attract groups up to thirty people. Other groups may be very small, perhaps with three or four participants.

Ideally, we advise hosts to aim for a group of eight to twelve regularly, which may mean they invite up to twenty people to join them. It is also important to stress continually that hosts should reach outside the church to invite those who are not part of a faith community.

However, if someone wants to do the study with only his or her immediate family, that's okay. In fact, we had nine-year-old Emma host her parents and siblings because the adults said their schedules were too busy. She would take time weekly to preview the video, look up the scriptures, and then select questions that she thought the whole family could discuss. She was the host facilitator in her own home. That's pretty cool.

By loosening the definition of leadership and lowering the training expectations, you will be able to put solid Christian resources into many people's hands. Then as they begin to invite, the momentum happens! It is the wonder of organic growth.

Many leaders want to play matchmaker when it comes to putting people into groups. Resist this urge! Let it happen organically. Remember, you can structure for control or growth but not both. Most healthy things grow. You don't have to tell a baby or a plant to grow. You give it a healthy environment and provide the basic food and water, and it grows. Given a healthy environment, most community groups form and grow organically also. In other words, people find their way to a group that fits their time schedule and life setting. In the G3 system most community groups will form simply by having the host invite their own neighbors, family, and coworkers. Relax, and let it happen, naturally.

But what about the people who didn't grab a resource and haven't been asked to join a group? Yes, the system adapts for those folks too. It's not a large issue. In a church with about three thousand in attendance each weekend, we have only a few dozen of these placement needs arise during each church-wide series. Although we don't want to play matchmaker, we do need a process for the people who need or request a recommendation. Perhaps they've just moved to the area, or they are socially shy and need help connecting with a group. To assist in these scenarios, create a listing of "safe" or proven groups. By safe, we mean the hosts you can confidently recommend as facilitators, who are spiritually mature, have been through a background check, and have experienced church training. We have twenty-five groups on this list out of more than three hundred, so it's a proportional need for your setting. In a church of one hundred, you may need two or three community groups to recommend for people who are not yet in a group.

It is wise to include smaller community groups with a healthy welcoming atmosphere on your list. It is intimidating for new people to come into a large group or into a group that has been meeting together for years. Smaller groups, however, tend to help new people feel welcome. It is also easier to follow up when someone is absent in groups that are smaller.

Step #6: Grow Together

This is where God takes over. As the groups begin to meet, growth begins. People learn each other's stories. They eat together. They laugh, and sometimes they cry. They bring meals to each other during times of celebration and times of sadness. With your encouragement, they will begin to take on new ministries within the church and accomplish great mission out in the world. And with time, they will begin to hold each other accountable for holy living.

As the groups begin to meet, put your emphasis on helping them establish healthy dynamics. Touch base with the host to encourage them and help troubleshoot any issues they may be having. Since there has not been any formal training, your hosts may need some guidance for handling people who dominate discussion or for responding to difficult questions. This is usually best done one-on-one and can usually be accomplished in a brief conversation.

Another goal during this season is to help each group maintain the balance we discussed in chapter 2. Develop a simple system to remind groups to spend time each week: praying (worship), serving (ministry), inviting (evangelism), studying (discipleship), and having fun together (fellowship). Each of these practices really is an important element to the healthy community group.

Step #7: Communicate What's Next

Momentum is a crazy experience. It can work for you or against you. The Grab, Gather, and Grow system can help you create momentum in your church. By putting easy-to-use tools into the hands of regular attendees, and by giving them the power to invite and host, you will surely have some initial growth. But then what?

Keep it going. By planning your church calendar and emphasizing key times of the year for church-wide studies, you will help keep this catalytic growth going. As previously suggested, you may want to introduce G3 series two or three times a year at these strategic moments: the first of the year, after Easter, and then when school starts in the fall. These are seasons of the year that people often engage in new ways.

As each (school) semester winds down, allow people to take a break, tell their success stories, and let them know when the next study will be ready. Most groups start looking for what they will do next anyway. So by building in a rhythm to your church calendar, it will help them know how to plan and probably even be a relief that you have done some of the work for them.

To build momentum into your *first* G3 series you might want to plan to roll out *two* church-wide series back-to-back. Go straight into a second one as soon as the first one is finished. Again, you don't want to do this all the time. But when trying to build initial momentum, you may want to keep the excitement going for two or three series in a row and then take a break.

Once a series is done, don't collect the DVDs. Instead, ask people to circulate the DVD and possibly even their participant guides to their unchurched friends. It's amazing how far-reaching this sharing can become.

This past Easter, as I was greeting people on the plaza of our church, a little girl came up to me and said, "Hey, you're the lady on our TV when my mommy opens her Bible." So I asked,

"Is your mommy in one of our community groups?" She replied, "Oh no. We don't go to church. But my aunt gave a DVD to my mom and told her she should watch it. Then my mom said, 'You know, if we ever go to church, we should check this place out.' So here we are."

Instead of asking people to return their materials to the church, encourage them to give them to their unchurched friends along with an invitation to weekend worship. This, too, has been an unexpected benefit to the G3 system.

CHAPTER 5

Dealing with Traditional Systems

The G3 process can bring you tremendous growth in many areas, but, as discussed previously, in each church situation there will be obstacles. One common concern is how to handle and align existing systems—and potentially competing systems for discipleship—within the church structure. Let's address three of these approaches to help you dream about ways to make G3 work in your setting.

Sunday School

It's not a new question: "Do you have Sunday school, or do you implement small groups?" The question behind the question seems to be: "Are you stuck with the rut of Sunday school, or have you moved forward into a small-group system?"

In many churches, some growing and some declining, there is a belief that small groups should be preferred over the Sunday school model. However, the truth is not that simple. Both systems have great qualities. In both systems, spiritual health and growth are desired. If you have a vital, alive Sunday school system that is producing numeric and spiritual growth, then consider incorporating the G3 system into it.

If, however, you have a Sunday school system that is not open to growth and producing changed hearts and lives, or is perhaps insulated into closed groups, you need to consider carefully the best way to proceed. One way to move forward is to set up a small-group system that functions outside of the Sunday morning education hour. That way Sunday school could continue while you introduce the G3 system as a distinct small-group campaign for the whole church (perhaps twice a year). As you evaluate the health of your Sunday school, consider whether or not that system is reaching into the community strategically to reach those who are far from God. Also, consider whether or not the Sunday school is moving attendees toward meaningful ministry in the church and mission in the community.

You as a leader must consider what system will work best in your setting to produce maturing followers of Christ. Don't fall into a *status quo* mentality, even if it means wisely challenging current systems.

Midweek Services

Many churches offer midweek and Sunday evening services. In some cases this is a strategic way of ministering to the congregation and the community. However, in other situations it continues simply because it's the way things have always been done. Do these services connect people in meaningful ways? Do new people come to Christ through these ministries? As you consider how best to reach the people of your community with the gospel of Christ, and how to connect them into small-group settings, make sure that your plans and systems are designed strategically to fulfill the purposes of Christ. Consider how your current ministries, including Sunday school and midweek services, are consuming resources of time, energy, and money. If they are not strategically fulfilling the purposes of the church, then as leaders it's up to us to change them.

In the early years of our church we began a midweek service, which we called Oasis. We had music and Bible teaching and even broke into smaller groups for discussion, at times. The crowd grew, and pretty soon we had about two hundred people meeting weekly. It seemed effective.

Soon, however, we realized that those attending the midweek service had stopped attending their community group. We had gone from about five hundred people engaged in weekly home groups, to two hundred involved in a midweek service. It was a painful decision, but we ended our midweek service. Oasis was a competing system with our greater goal of involving every person in a weekly community group. There will be times in ministry where leaders must make difficult decisions. As Jim Collins says, "Good is the enemy of great."[2]

Affinity Groups

As you consider the G3 process, you may also want to give thought to affinity groups, such as men's groups, women's studies, and singles' groups. We do not organize and promote these gatherings. Instead, like all of the G3 groups, we allow them to form organically.

If you have a long-running history of affinity groups within your church structure, you may have to treat them somewhat like the Sunday school. Do we incorporate these into the G3 system or let them orbit? Some men invite only their guy friends. Some young moms invite others like themselves. There is no need for us to intervene and create these settings; they naturally occur based on what people perceive their needs to be and what their schedules allow.

In our situation, we have incorporated all groups into the G3 system with one exception: studies for brand-new believers. We steer them toward a seven-week course that introduces them to the Christian faith and answers basic issues of the faith. At the conclusion of this course, we then assimilate them into the overall body of the church through the G3 process.

---

2. Jim Collins, *Good to Great: Why Some Companies Make the Leap . . . and Others Don't* (New York: HarperBusiness, 2001).

CHAPTER 6

The G3 Timeline

6 months to G3 launch:	• Pastor and lay leadership commit to a curriculum and date. • Leadership teams are selected to handle ordering, distribution, and follow-up.
3 months to G3 launch:	• Materials are ordered. • Follow-up letters to hosts are written in advance. • Promotional materials for the series are designed.
3 weeks to G3 launch:	• The pastor casts the vision for G3 and invites people to Grab, Gather, and Grow.
2 weeks to G3 launch:	• Cast the vision again. Materials are made available to grab after the service. • Host cards are filled out at curriculum tables. • Hosts begin inviting and gathering their crowd. • Letters, phone calls, and e-mails go out to encourage hosts.

1 week to G3 launch:	• Cast the vision again. Materials are available to grab after the service. • Host cards are filled out at curriculum tables. • Hosts continue to gather a crowd. • Letters, phone calls, and e-mails go out to encourage hosts.
Launch service:	• Sermon series begins. • Materials continue to be available. Host cards can still be filled out. • Hosts continue to invite and gather for their group. • Letters, phone calls, and e-mails go out. • Groups begin this week!
Week 2 of series:	• Groups continue to form. Have materials and host cards available. • Continue the follow-up process with hosts. • Check in with hosts to see how week 1 went. • Encourage groups to share openly and take on a mission project.
Week 3 or 4 of series:	• Check in with hosts to help them troubleshoot. • Finalize plans for a mission project. • Encourage them to select another study and keep meeting together. • Remind groups to do a fun social activity together.

CHAPTER 7

Getting Started

Did you catch the vision? Are you excited about the possibilities in your community? You can do this!

It will work in your setting with the right planning and execution. In your setting, to help some of the leaders get on board with the concept, we suggest that your team watch the *Grab, Gather, Grow* video together (available on DVD or streaming from Cokesbury.com). You may want to buy a few copies of this book to put into their hands so that they can digest it and begin to dream along with you. By sharing and multiplying the vision, you will be more likely to have a successful G3 launch.

It will also be important to have an idea of how to begin. We suggest that you obtain a copy of the community-group launch experience, *Living the Five*, which is available from most bookstores. This five-week study will help your groups launch because it is based on the Great Commission and Great Commandment. The content focuses on how to build health into the church, into the community-group structure, and into our personal lives. Using this study to launch the G3 process may help you build in a healthy balance right from the start.

Remember, you are a leader, and leaders have the responsibility of casting vision and gaining new ground. So as you move forward, we encourage you to stay positive. Will you have obstacles? Yes. Will there be people who don't want to support your vision? Most likely. But move forward anyway. Great leaders think *when*, not *if*; they say *so*, not *but*.

Friends, you can do this, and we believe Jesus will use you to change your church and community through the process. Stay close to Christ. Stay humble. Stay focused on the Great Commandment. Be kind, and lead well.

Session One, *Living the Five*

CONTENTS

APPENDICES

COMMUNITY GROUP LEADERS

FOREWORD

BY RICK WARREN

Jim and Jen Cowart planted a church in 2001, and I watched this church every year grow stronger, grow deeper, grow healthier, grow larger, and grow more visionary. In fact, this church is one of Saddleback's Church Health Award winners! We are pretty picky about the churches that we honor because they must be balanced in worship, in fellowship, in discipleship, in ministry, and in evangelism. They are doing the purposes of God through the processes that balance all of these things. They have the strategy and the structure that allow them to grow year after year after year.

What does it mean to be purpose driven?

We believe, and the Bible teaches in Acts 2, John 17, Ephesians 4, and other places, that God wants your church to be built around God's eternal purposes. There are five of those purposes—not four, not six, not seven. They are modeled by the church in Acts 2; they are prayed for by Jesus in John 17; they are explained by Paul in Ephesians 4; but they are best seen in the Great Commandment and the Great Commission. We believe that a great commitment to the Great Commandment and the Great Commission will grow a great church. This is no theory, friend; this works. We've seen it work in rural areas, urban areas, and suburban areas, and regardless of the size or the denomination of your church, you can be built around the purposes of God.

INTRODUCTION

Welcome to Living the Five!

Whether you've been a Christ follower for years or you're just checking out the Christian faith for the very first time—welcome! This five-week study is designed to give you new insights into the Bible, how it applies to us, and what it looks like to live it out.

Each week you'll have opportunities to share your own ideas and experiences, watch a short video teaching on that week's theme, discuss the scriptures, learn from each other, and build relationships with others in your group. There's also lots of extra material if you want to really dig in, including options for further study and questions for life application.

At the end of each session, you will find daily devotions that will allow you to slow down and reflect on God's promises and precepts. You will then have a chance to respond by journaling. By doing this study, you'll be learning with a large group in church, a small group in a living room, and alone with God on your own.

We're excited about what God has in store for you and your group over the next five weeks, and we're praying that you will experience God in a fresh way as a result of this study.

Jim and Jennifer Cowart

YOU CAN'T DO LIFE

ALONE

One of the first things Jesus did when he began his earthly ministry was recruit a ragtag bunch of fishermen, tax collectors, and others to hang out with him. These ordinary people went on to do extraordinary things as Jesus's disciples, but in the beginning they were simply Jesus's friends and, in a way, his small group.

If Jesus needed to walk through life with other people, we definitely do. Yet so often we isolate ourselves, leaving ourselves open to temptation, loneliness, and all kinds of negative influences and bad decisions. We're stronger when we're not alone. God created us to need each other as we live out our commitment to Jesus.

> IF JESUS NEEDED TO WALK THROUGH LIFE WITH OTHER PEOPLE, WE DEFINITELY DO.

Not only that, doing life together is just more fun! As we build relationships with other Christ-followers, we can encourage each other, pray for each other, laugh together, and learn together. Christian music artist Sara Groves says these relationships make life "half as hard and twice as good."* That's what we want for each one of you, in this community group and in our church, and it's the focus of today's session.

* Sara Groves, vocal performance of "Twice as Good," by Christa Wells and Sara Groves, recorded on *Fireflies and Songs*, released 2009, Kiss Me Not Publishing and Sara Groves Music.

SHARE YOUR STORY

EACH OF US HAS A STORY. THE EVENTS OF OUR LIVES— GOOD, BAD, WONDERFUL, OR CHALLENGING—HAVE SHAPED WHO WE ARE.

GOD KNOWS YOUR STORY, AND GOD INTENDS TO REDEEM IT—TO USE EVERY STRUGGLE AND EVERY JOY TO ULTIMATELY BRING YOU INTO RELATIONSHIP WITH GOD. WHEN WE SHARE OUR STORIES WITH OTHERS, WE GIVE THEM THE OPPORTUNITY TO SEE GOD AT WORK.

WHEN WE SHARE OUR STORIES, WE ALSO REALIZE WE ARE NOT ALONE— THAT WE HAVE COMMON EXPERIENCES AND THOUGHTS AND THAT OTHERS CAN UNDERSTAND WHAT WE ARE GOING THROUGH. YOUR STORY CAN ENCOURAGE SOMEONE ELSE. AND TELLING IT CAN LEAD TO A PATH OF FREEDOM FOR YOU AND FOR THOSE YOU SHARE IT WITH.

- Open your group with prayer. This should be a brief, simple prayer in which you invite God to give you insight as you study. You can pray for specific requests at the end of the meeting, or stop momentarily to pray if a particular situation comes up during your discussion.

- Before you start this first meeting, get contact information for every participant. Take time to pass around a copy of the Community Group Roster on page 86, a sheet of paper, or your personal Partici-pant Guide, opened to the Community Group Roster. Ask someone to make copies or type up a list with everyone's information and e-mail it to the group during the week.

1. **WHAT BROUGHT YOU HERE? WHAT DO YOU HOPE TO GET OUT OF THIS GROUP?**

2. **WHAT'S YOUR USUAL APPROACH TO MEETING NEW PEOPLE?**
   A. **TO BE HONEST, IT'S PRETTY SCARY FOR ME.**
   B. **I'M CAUTIOUS AT FIRST, BUT WHEN I FEEL COMFORTABLE I OPEN UP.**
   C. **I'VE NEVER REALLY MET A STRANGER—WHAT DO YOU WANT TO KNOW?!**

Whether your group is new or ongoing, it's always important to reflect on and review your values together. On page 83 is a Community Group Covenant with the values we've found most useful in sustaining healthy, balanced groups. We recommend that you choose one or two values—ones you haven't previously focused on or have room to grow in—to emphasize during this study. Choose ones that will take your group to the next stage of intimacy and spiritual health.

We recommend you rotate host homes on a regular basis and let the hosts lead the meeting. Studies show that healthy groups rotate leadership. This helps to develop every member's ability to shepherd a few people in a safe environment. Even Jesus gave others the opportunity to serve alongside him (Mark 6:30-44). Look at the Frequent Questions in the appendix for additional information about hosting or leading the group.

TAKE TIME TO GET TO KNOW EACH OTHER. INTRODUCE EVERYONE—YOU MAY EVEN WANT TO HAVE NAME TAGS FOR YOUR FIRST MEETING.

The Community Group Calendar on page 85 is a tool for planning who will host and lead each meeting. Take a few minutes to plan hosts and leaders for your remaining meetings. Don't skip this important step! It will revolutionize your group.

WATCH
THE DVD

- Write down key thoughts, questions, and things you want to remember or talk about together.

- After watching the video, have someone read the discussion questions in the Hear God's Story section and direct the discussion among the group.

- As you go through each of the subsequent sections, ask someone else to read the questions and direct the discussion.

HEAR GOD'S STORY

SOME PEOPLE THINK "EMOTION WILL SUSTAIN DEVOTION"—THAT CHRISTIANITY IS A MATTER OF MOVING FROM ONE SPIRITUAL HIGH TO THE NEXT AND THAT IF YOU CAN SUSTAIN THESE FEELINGS IT WILL BE EASY TO FOLLOW CHRIST.

UNFORTUNATELY, LIFE IS SOMETIMES HARD, AND IT'S UNREALISTIC TO EXPECT YOUR EMOTIONS TO DRIVE YOUR SPIRITUAL LIFE. INSTEAD, YOU NEED TO BE GROUNDED IN GOD'S WORD, IN DAILY COMMUNICATION WITH GOD IN PRAYER, AND IN CONNECTION TO OTHER BELIEVERS WHO CAN STRENGTHEN YOUR FAITH. LIFE IS FULL OF MOUNTAINS AND VALLEYS, BUT GOD DESIGNED US TO TRAVEL THE PATH TOGETHER.

READ 1 SAMUEL 20:12-13, 16-17

*Then Jonathan told David, "I pledge by the L*ORD *God of Israel that I will question my father by this time tomorrow or on the third day. If he seems favorable toward David, I will definitely send word and make sure you know. But if my father intends to harm you, then may the L*ORD *deal harshly with me, Jonathan, and worse still if I don't tell you right away so that you can escape safely. May the L*ORD *be with you as he once was with my father. . . .*

*"If Jonathan's name is also eliminated, then the L*ORD *will seek retribution from David!" So Jonathan again made a pledge to David because he loved David as much as himself (CEB).*

1. **WHY DO YOU THINK JONATHAN WAS SO WILLING TO HELP DAVID, EVEN AT A COST TO HIMSELF?**

2. **HOW HAD THE LORD BEEN WITH JONATHAN'S FATHER, SAUL?**

3. **JONATHAN'S STATEMENT IN VERSE 16 IMPLICATES SAUL AS ONE OF DAVID'S ENEMIES. WHY WOULD JONATHAN MAKE A SOLEMN PLEDGE AGAINST HIS OWN FATHER?**

4. **IN ANCIENT CULTURES, IF BOTH PARTIES REPEATED THE TERMS IT MADE A SOLEMN PLEDGE UNBREAKABLE. WHAT INSIGHT DOES THIS GIVE YOU INTO VERSE 17?**

STUDY NOTES

IN THE VIDEO, JIM AND JENNIFER QUOTED HEBREWS 10:24, WHICH SAYS WE ARE TO "SPUR" ONE ANOTHER ON (NIV).

EVEN IF YOU'VE NEVER RIDDEN A HORSE, YOU'RE PROBABLY FAMILIAR WITH SPURS FROM THE MOVIES. BASICALLY THEY ARE JUST SMALL METAL TOOLS A RIDER WEARS ON HIS OR HER BOOTS, AND WHEN THE RIDER WANTS TO URGE THE HORSE TO WALK OR RUN MORE QUICKLY OR MOVE FROM SIDE TO SIDE, HE OR SHE GENTLY PUSHES THE SPUR INTO THE HORSE'S SIDE.

WHEN USED CORRECTLY A SPUR DOES NOT HURT THE HORSE, BUT IT CAN BE A GREAT WAY TO REINFORCE THE RIDER'S OTHER COMMANDS OR COMMUNICATE QUICKLY AND CLEARLY DURING RIDING.

In addition to the wonderful metaphor of this verse, which gives us a word picture of urging each other on to do better, it's also one of many verses in the Bible you just can't obey if you don't participate in the life of a church and connect with other believers.

HERE ARE A FEW MORE:

Love each other like the members of your family. Be the best at showing honor to each other.
Romans 12:10 (CEB)

Serve each other through love.
Galatians 5:13 (CEB)

Be kind, compassionate, and forgiving to each other, in the same way God forgave you in Christ.
Ephesians 4:32 (CEB)

CREATE A NEW STORY

GOD WANTS YOU TO BE PART OF GOD'S KINGDOM—TO WEAVE YOUR STORY INTO GOD'S.

THAT WILL MEAN CHANGE—TO GO GOD'S WAY RATHER THAN YOUR OWN. THIS WON'T HAPPEN OVERNIGHT, BUT IT SHOULD HAPPEN STEADILY. BY STARTING WITH SMALL, SIMPLE CHOICES, WE BEGIN TO CHANGE OUR DIRECTION.

THE HOLY SPIRIT HELPS US ALONG THE WAY—GIVING US GIFTS TO SERVE THE BODY, OFFERING US INSIGHTS INTO SCRIPTURE, AND CHALLENGING US TO LOVE NOT ONLY THOSE AROUND US BUT THOSE FAR FROM GOD.

IN THIS SECTION, TALK ABOUT HOW YOU WILL APPLY THE WIS-
DOM YOU'VE LEARNED FROM THE TEACHING AND BIBLE STUDY.
THEN THINK ABOUT PRACTICAL STEPS YOU CAN TAKE IN THE
COMING WEEK TO LIVE OUT WHAT YOU'VE LEARNED.

1. HAVE YOU EVER MADE BAD DECISIONS WHEN YOU WERE ALONE? HOW
   WOULD THE PRESENCE OF OTHER PEOPLE WHO CARED ABOUT YOU PO-
   TENTIALLY HAVE MADE A DIFFERENCE IN THOSE SITUATIONS?

2. IS IT INTIMIDATING OR SCARY TO THINK OF LETTING YOUR GROUP GET TO
   KNOW THE REAL YOU?

3. HAVE YOU ISOLATED YOURSELF IN ANY AREA OF LIFE? WHAT STEPS CAN
   YOU TAKE TO BEGIN SHARING THAT PART OF YOUR LIFE WITH OTHERS?

4. WHAT ARE SOME CONCRETE WAYS YOU CAN SPUR EACH OTHER ON THIS
   WEEK?

5. TAKE A LOOK AT THE SEGMENTS BELOW AND WRITE THE NAMES OF TWO OR THREE PEOPLE YOU KNOW. COMMIT TO PRAYING FOR GOD'S GUIDANCE AND AN OPPORTUNITY TO SHARE WITH EACH OF THEM. PERHAPS THEY WOULD BE OPEN TO JOINING THE GROUP? SHARE YOUR LISTS WITH THE GROUP SO YOU CAN ALL BE PRAYING FOR THE PEOPLE YOU'VE IDENTIFIED.

FAMILY (immediate or extended)	
FAMILIAR (neighbors, kids' sports teams, school, and so forth)	
FRIENDS	
FUN (gym, hobbies, hangouts)	
FIRM (work)	

6. CONSIDER SOMEONE—IN THIS GROUP OR OUTSIDE IT—THAT YOU CAN BEGIN GOING DEEPER WITH IN AN INTENTIONAL WAY. THIS MIGHT BE YOUR MOM OR DAD, A COUSIN, AN AUNT OR UNCLE, A ROOMMATE, A COLLEGE BUDDY, OR A NEIGHBOR. CHOOSE SOMEONE WHO MIGHT BE OPEN TO "DOING LIFE" WITH YOU AT A DEEPER LEVEL, AND PRAY ABOUT THAT OPPORTUNITY.

7. THIS WEEK, HOW WILL YOU INTERACT WITH THE BIBLE? CAN YOU COMMIT TO SPENDING TIME IN DAILY PRAYER OR STUDY OF GOD'S WORD (USE THE DAILY DEVOTIONS SECTION TO GUIDE YOU)? TELL THE GROUP HOW YOU PLAN TO FOLLOW JESUS THIS WEEK, AND THEN, AT YOUR NEXT MEETING, TALK ABOUT YOUR PROGRESS AND CHALLENGES.

8. STACK YOUR HANDS (LIKE A SPORTS TEAM DOES IN THE HUDDLE) AND COMMIT TO TAKING A RISK AND GOING DEEPER IN YOUR GROUP AND IN YOUR RELATIONSHIPS WITH EACH OTHER.

9. TO CLOSE YOUR TIME TOGETHER, SPEND SOME TIME WORSHIPPING GOD TOGETHER—PRAYING, SINGING, READING SCRIPTURE.

- Have someone use his or her musical gifts to lead the group in a worship song. Try singing a cappella, using a worship CD, or having someone accompany your singing with a musical instrument.

- Choose a psalm or other favorite verse, and read it aloud together. Make it a time of praise and worship, as the words remind you of all God has done for you.

- Ask, "How can we pray for you this week?" Invite everyone to share, but don't force the issue. Be sure to write prayer requests on your Prayer Requests and Praise Reports (page 87).

- Close your meeting with prayer.

DIGGING DEEPER

IF YOU FEEL GOD NUDGING YOU TO GO DEEPER, TAKE SOME TIME BEFORE THE NEXT MEETING TO DIG INTO GOD'S WORD.

EXPLORE THE BIBLE PASSAGES RELATED TO THIS SESSION'S THEME ON YOUR OWN, AND JOT YOUR REFLECTIONS IN A JOURNAL OR IN THIS STUDY GUIDE.

A GREAT WAY TO GAIN INSIGHT ON A PASSAGE IS TO READ IT IN SEVERAL DIFFERENT TRANSLATIONS.

YOU MAY WANT TO USE A BIBLE APP OR WEBSITE TO COMPARE TRANSLATIONS.

READ JOHN 15:12-17

1. WE WILL PROBABLY NEVER BE REQUIRED TO PHYSICALLY DIE FOR A FRIEND. WHAT ELSE COULD JESUS MEAN WHEN HE CALLS US TO LAY DOWN OUR LIVES FOR EACH OTHER?

2. JESUS TELLS HIS DISCIPLES TWICE TO LOVE EACH OTHER. IN THE MIDDLE OF THOSE TWO COMMANDS HE REMINDS THEM TO OBEY AND DO WHAT HE'S ASKED. WHAT'S THE CONNECTION BETWEEN THE TWO?

3. WHAT ARE SOME OF THE THINGS JESUS LEARNED FROM THE FATHER THAT HE PASSED ALONG TO HIS FOLLOWERS?

READ ROMANS 12:9-21

1. THIS PASSAGE IS FULL OF INSTRUCTIONS FOR LIVING IN COMMUNITY WITH OTHER BELIEVERS. WHICH ONE DO YOU FIND MOST CHALLENGING?

2. WHAT DOES VERSE 11 TELL US IS THE KEY TO KEEPING OUR SPIRITUAL FERVOR?

3. WHAT ARE SOME WAYS WE CAN REJOICE WITH THOSE WHO REJOICE? MOURN WITH THOSE WHO MOURN?

DAILY DEVOTIONALS

Day 1 • Read Proverbs 13:20

Walk with wise people and become wise; befriend fools and get in trouble (CEB).

RESPOND

How do we grow in wisdom just by associating with other wise people? Why is the opposite also true?

DAY 2 • READ ROMANS 15:7

So welcome each other, in the same way that Christ also welcomed you, for God's glory (CEB).

RESPOND

What are some ways Christ accepted you? How can you show that same acceptance to others?

DAY 3 • READ ECCLESIASTES 4:9-10

Two are better than one because they have a good return for their hard work. If either should fall, one can pick up the other. But how miserable are those who fall and don't have a companion to help them up! (CEB).

RESPOND

Have you ever "fallen" and needed a friend's help? How could you be that friend to someone else? Ask God for opportunities to love other people this way.

DAY 4 • READ PHILIPPIANS 2:1-2

Therefore, if there is any encouragement in Christ, any comfort in love, any sharing in the Spirit, any sympathy, complete my joy by thinking the same way, having the same love, being united, and agreeing with each other (CEB).

RESPOND

Do people always have to agree? How does the rest of the scripture passage explain this command?

DAY 5 • READ 1 JOHN 3:18

Little children, let's not love with words or speech but with action and truth.

RESPOND

What is the difference between these two kinds of love? How can we love with actions and truth?

DAY 6

Use the following space to write any thoughts God has put in your heart and mind about the things we have looked at in this session and during your Daily Devotions time this week.

_____

_____

_____

_____

_____

9 781501 825057